D0906817

WORLD WAR II

The Full Story

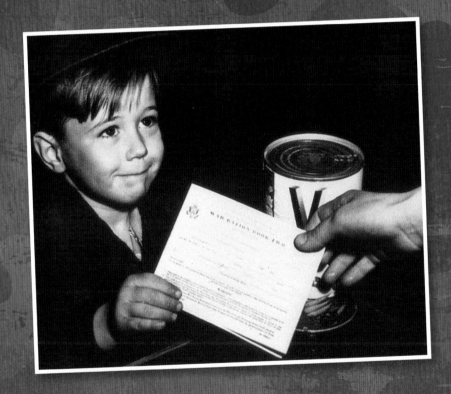

Home Fronts

Published by Brown Bear Books Ltd
4877 N. Circulo Bujia
Tucson, AZ 85718
USA

and

First Floor
9-17 St. Albans Place
London N1 0NX

ISBN: 978-1-78121-232-5

Library of Congress Cataloging-in-Publication
Data available upon request

Managing Editor: Tim Cooke
Designer: Lynne Lennon
Picture Manager: Sophie Mortimer
Editorial Director: Lindsey Lowe
Design Manager: Keith Davis
Children's Publisher: Anne O'Daly
Production Director: Alastair Gourlay

Manufactured in the United States of America

CPSIA compliance information: Batch# AG/5566

CONTENTS

INTRODUCTION

World War II (1939–1945) was the first truly global war. It had an impact on most countries in the world. Its effects were felt on the home fronts as well as on the front lines. Many countries suffered from fighting or bombing, or from enemy occupation. Of the approximately 60 million people who died in the war, nearly two-thirds were civilians. They died as a result of enemy bombing or occupation, or from starvation or disease.

With France and the Low Countries—the Netherlands, Belgium, and Luxembourg—under German rule, the major Allied home fronts were in the United States, Britain, and the Soviet Union. On the other side, both German and Italian civilians found their lives greatly changed.

The War Effort

In many ways, the war was an industrial battle. The major combatants changed their economies to produce weapons, ammunition, and other hardware. Everyone was expected to make a contribution to the war effort, even at the cost of individual freedoms. The economic changes led to shortages of food and

⬆ In the absence of rifles, men from the British Home Guard go through a drill using sticks.

→ This famous image of Uncle Sam was painted by James Montgomery Flagg to encourage Americans to join the army.

other materials, and to a huge rise in the numbers of women working in factories or on farms. Life was particularly hard in countries under German or Japanese occupation. Some people willingly collaborated with the invaders, while others joined resistance groups. Most people simply tried to carry on with their lives.

In Europe, meanwhile, the Germans set out to exterminate "inferior" peoples—including Jews—in a campaign of mass murder known as the Holocaust.

U.S. HOME FRONT

When the United States entered the war, it changed the lives of everyone in the country, even though America did not experience any fighting on its own soil.

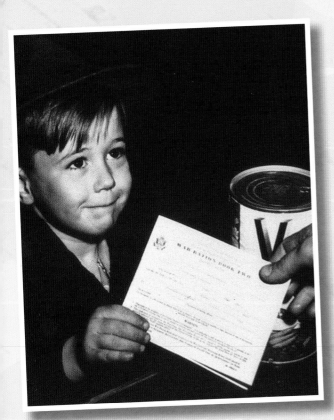

↑ A young boy uses his ration book to buy goods. Most foods and a range of other goods were rationed.

The United States was one of the few major combatants to escape military action at home, although U.S. territories in Hawaii and Alaska were attacked. However, the war still affected life in many ways. Even while the United States was technically neutral at the start of the war, it was closely involved in the conflict. President Franklin D. Roosevelt had enabled U.S. industry to supply material and financial aid to the Allies.

The United States Enters the War

Things changed when the Japanese Imperial Fleet attacked Pearl Harbor in Hawaii on December 7, 1941. Roosevelt declared war on Japan the next day. When Germany declared war against the United States on December 11, the nation was suddenly fighting on two fronts, against Japan in the Pacific and against Germany and Italy in Europe. The Pearl Harbor attack caused panic in the United States. Cities took precautions against enemy air raids. On the West Coast,

↑ New Yorkers stand in line outside a school to collect their wartime ration books.

communities worried about enemy troop landings or acts of sabotage. Americans were scared but also angry. They saw themselves as having suffered an unprovoked attack. The sense of outrage fueled a determination to win the war.

Life Changes

Despite Americans' high standard of living, the war effort still required dramatic changes to their daily lives. They had to consume less and produce more. To control the distribution of goods, Roosevelt established the Office of Price Administration (OPA). It imposed strict

KEY THEMES

OFFICE OF CIVILIAN DEFENSE

New York mayor Fiorello H. La Guardia organized the Office of Civilian Defense in 1941. Its task was to organize a national system of air-raid warnings and shelters in case of air attack, and a system of blackouts to confuse enemy bombers. Volunteers were coordinated by the First Lady, Eleanor Roosevelt, before she resigned under pressure from her husband's political opponents.

→ Children buy tickets in a movie theater that also sells war bonds. All U.S. citizens were encouraged to buy bonds.

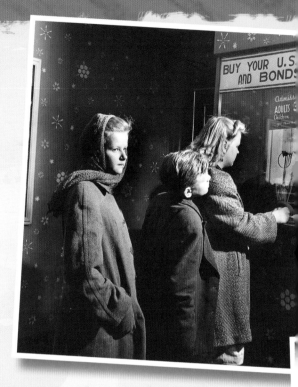

limits on prices and wages and rationed scarce goods: sugar, meat, butter, and canned goods. People could only buy a few gallons of gasoline a week, so automobile use fell dramatically.

The War Economy

Many Americans actually had more money during the war than in peacetime. This was partly due to rationing—there was less to spend money on—and partly because there were more jobs. The government targeted Americans' money

KEY PEOPLE

CELEBRITIES AND THE WAR

Americans serving in the war included Hollywood actors, musicians, and athletes. They included the bandleader Glenn Miller, actors James Stewart and Clark Gable, and major-league baseball players Ted Williams and Joe DiMaggio. Even animated stars served the cause: Bugs Bunny and Daffy Duck squared off against Hitler and the Japanese.

to help pay for the war. Income taxes rose sharply and the government also borrowed tens of millions of dollars through savings schemes known as war bonds. These were saving certificates through which Americans loaned their money to the government in return for a certain rate of interest when the conflict was over.

The Great Depression had lingered into the late 1930s. At the start of the war in Europe in September 1939, US employment was above 15 percent. By 1943, with the war economy in full swing, unemployment had fallen to just over 1 percent; the lowest level ever measured in the United States.

American companies switched from the production of consumer goods to military equipment: General Motors produced the M-4 Sherman tanks. The shipbuilding company of Henry Kaiser could build a cargo ship in just 80 hours. These so-called Liberty Ships were used to carry supplies across the Atlantic. American shipyards could build them at a faster rate than the German navy could sink them. By the middle of the war, the Allied armies and fleets knew that they outnumbered the enemy in every kind of military hardware. The workers on the home front made a significant contribution to that decisive edge.

New Forms of Equality

One positive outcome of the war in the United States was a movement toward racial and gender equality. In pre-war America, employment opportunities for

⬇ This photo shows a Boeing aircraft factory that has been switched to produce B-17 Flying Fortresses.

ZOOT SUIT RIOTS

The zoot suit, a long coat with baggy pants, was popular among young Mexican Americans in Los Angeles. Servicemen resented the youths, and tensions grew between the two groups. In June 1943 a rumor spread that a sailor had been beaten up by zoot suiters. More than 2,000 soldiers and sailors rampaged through East Los Angeles, beating up young Mexicans and tearing their zoot suits to shreds.

women were limited and African Americans and other minorities were treated poorly. The war changed this. Women went to work in factories and assembly lines, taking over male jobs as the men went to fight on the front line.

African Americans were recruited into the military but they were kept in segregated all-black units. Most were forbidden full-combat status. Hispanic Americans

and Native Americans were allowed to serve in integrated combat units. At home, the war industry relied on racial minorities. But in a country used to racial segregation, race riots broke out in Detroit and southern California as whites and non-whites worked closely together.

Japanese Americans

More than 100,000 Japanese Americans lived on the West Coast at the start of the war. After the bombing of Pearl Harbor, many Americans saw them as a threat to national security. In February 1942, Roosevelt issued Executive Order 9066. It ordered Japanese Americans to

➔ Americans of Japanese descent arrive at an assembly center in California in April 1942.

We Can Do It!

WAR PRODUCTION CO-ORDINATING COMMITTEE

← Rosie the Riveter appeared in poster campaigns to encourage women to work in industry.

leave coastal areas. They were forced to live in camps inland. The camps were like small towns, with their own newspapers and police forces. Most of the Japanese Americans were American citizens, born and raised in the United States. Many young Japanese Americans later enlisted in the military. The all-Japanese American 442nd Regimental Combat Team fought in Italy and became the U.S. Army's most decorated regiment.

JAPANESE INTERNMENT

Roosevelt's Executive Order 9066 forced Japanese Americans to move to internment camps. It mainly affected the West Coast, where most Japanese Americans lived. Although most of the Japanese were U.S. citizens, they lost their homes and businesses for good. Many spent years in the camps—including parents whose sons were fighting against Japan.

KEY THEMES

The War at Home

The air raids Americans feared never came. Rationing was inconvenient, but was never as harsh as in other countries. But American civilians still suffered some of the traumas of war. There were 14 million men in uniform, many of them serving overseas. Around 300,000 servicemen never returned.

Despite the changes to society, life carried on. Major-league baseball continued throughout the war. Hollywood produced patriotic movies. The South remained segregated, even for African Americans in military uniform.

↑ The Empire State Building rises above New York City in this view from 1945.

"On March 23, 1943, while in class at high school, two FBI agents arrested me. I was interned when I was seventeen and released when I was twenty-two. Without experiencing internment, no one can appreciate the intense terror of government power and the despair of hopelessness and endless time one feels."

Eberhard Fuhr
German-American student

Civilians were constantly reminded that they were at war. Propaganda posters reminded them not to reveal military secrets or urged them to meet their production targets.

The government carefully controlled the news reports and images of war their citizens received. The terror of the "real war" never made it into Hollywood movies or newsreels. But there were some exceptions. The public was shocked by the press images of dead Marines after U.S. forces captured the Pacific island of Tarawa in November 1943.

A New Country

The whole country changed during the war. In 1939, the United States was still suffering from the lingering effects of the Great Depression. By 1945, it was the wealthiest and most powerful nation on earth. Its birth rate was rising and Americans were increasingly optimistic about the future. While much of Europe and Asia lay in ruins, U.S. cities were full of gleaming new buildings that displayed the country's new prosperity.

A Different Country?

While the war had many hard sides—internment, censorship, and rationing—many Americans believed it also brought more positive benefits. There was a move toward social equality, and the creation of an economy with plenty of well-paid jobs. The war effort created new centers of growth, particularly in the South. Even during the war, a new majority, the "middle class," expected to enjoy a better life when the conflict was over than their parents had done, with home ownership, a car, and the promise of an even better life for their children.

➔ An African American worker inspects shell cases in a factory in Philadelphia.

ALLIED HOME FRONTS

The outbreak of war transformed almost every aspect of life for civilians. Everyone was expected to contribute something to the war effort.

On September 3, 1939, Prime Minister Neville Chamberlain made a radio broadcast to tell people that Britain was at war with Germany. The population prepared for the worst, but for the eight months that followed, little happened. The period became known as the "Phoney War."

The Phoney War

Even though no bombing had started, life in Britain changed immediately. City councils built thousands of concrete and brick shelters or dug air-raid shelters in local parks. In London, the platforms of the subways were used as shelters. People with backyards used outdoor shelters known as Anderson shelters. These were

➔ A British schoolteacher instructs his students during a gas-mask drill in September 1939.

TAKE THEM BACK!
TAKE THEM BACK!
TAKE THEM BACK!..

DON'T do it,
Mother—

LEAVE THE CHILDREN
WHERE THEY ARE

ISSUED BY THE MINISTRY OF HEALTH

← This British poster encourages city parents to leave their children in the safety of the countryside.

"Bombs flashed, then simmered down to pinpoints of dazzling white. These pinpoints would go out one by one as the unseen heroes of the moment smothered them with sand. But other pinpoints burned on and soon a yellow flame would leap up. They had done their work—another building was on fire."

Ernie Pyle
U.S. war correspondent,
London Blitz, 1940

shelters constructed from corrugated iron and half-buried in the ground. About 2.25 million Anderson shelters were given to households by the government.

When the bombing began, it was found that Anderson shelters sometimes collapsed under direct hits. They were replaced with Morrison shelters in 1941. These were indoor shelters made from very strong iron; they could be used as tables when there were no air raids. A Morrison shelter could withstand tons of

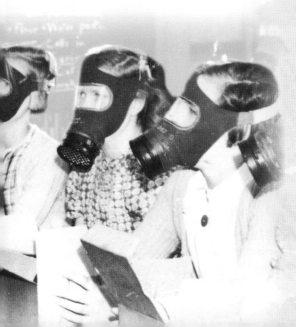

rubble falling on top of it. The shelters saved thousands of lives. All civilians—even babies—were issued with gas masks in case of attacks using poison gas.

A blackout was introduced to stop German bombers using light on the ground to guide them toward their targets. People were ordered to put heavy shutters over windows, and all street lights were switched off. Cars could only use sidelights. Initially the number of road accidents rose so dramatically that the blackout conditions had be relaxed.

Life in the Blitz

By the middle of 1940, the Phoney War was over. German U-boats had sunk large numbers of Allied merchant ships in the Atlantic, which resulted in food shortages in Britain. Strict food rationing was introduced for the first time.

When German air raids began on Britain in 1940, the Luftwaffe (German air force) initially attacked military targets, but from September, it began a series of night raids on key industrial cities. The raids were known as the Blitz. London, Coventry, Plymouth, and Sheffield were heavily bombed. Their citizens spent the night in air-raid shelters and emerged every morning to see if their houses were

⬇ Londoners examine an Anderson shelter after a German bomb made a crater right next to it.

→ A British poster urges people to recycle food waste to feed farmyard animals.

We want your **KITCHEN WASTE**

PIG FOOD

KEEP IT DRY, FREE FROM GLASS, BONES, METAL, PAPER, ETC. IT ALSO FEEDS POULTRY... *YOUR COUNCIL WILL COLLECT*

still standing. Between 1939 and 1945, 60,595 people were killed in air raids. More than one million city children were evacuated, or sent to the countryside, to live with strangers. While the experience was often traumatic for the children and their parents, evacuation meant that only 7,736 children were killed in air raids.

Workforce Changes

In May 1940 the Military Powers Act put the government in control of all employment in the country. Women aged between 18 and 50 went to work in agriculture and industry, doing jobs usually done by men. Women worked as welders, farmers, and bus drivers, and on the railroads.

RATIONING IN BRITAIN

By 1941 virtually every commodity was rationed in Britain. Most items could only be bought using official ration coupons. Soap, paper, new clothing, and gasoline were all restricted. The government encouraged people to cut down on all types of consumption. Another campaign urged Britons to "Dig for Victory" by growing fruit and vegetables. Food such as meat, eggs, and butter were rationed, which helped to ensure everyone had a balanced diet. But many families had contacts who would find them a little extra—but at a high cost.

KEY THEMES

→ During the war, production at this fighter plane factory in central Britain increased by more than 700 percent.

The Women's Land Army was formed in 1939 to grow food and raise livestock. It had 80,000 members by 1944. More than 400,000 women worked in civil defense roles, and around two million women made weapons or ammunition for the military.

The need to keep industry working was so great that one in every ten British men who was drafted was not sent to the military services but to work in Britain's coalmines. They were known as Bevin's Boys, for the minister of labor, Ernest Bevin. Conditions were terrible, accidents were frequent, and miners went on strike, leading to a fall in coal production between 1942 and 1945. In the factories, however, the output of military hardware rose dramatically.

Britain's industrial achievements were huge. Despite relying on overseas supplies, largely from the United States, the British were able to cope with enemy action and shortages, distribute food and other goods fairly, and see their industrial production rise. Some historians call the wartime period Britain's "finest hour."

The Soviet Home Front

Life was already hard in the Soviet Union before the war began. Under the communist leader, Joseph Stalin, farmers were grouped together into large "collectives" to grow crops. The system was inefficient and did not produce enough food. The policy helped cause a famine that killed as many as 15 million Soviet peasants.

When Germany invaded the Soviet Union in June 1941, the country had prepared for a possible war. In just six months Soviet factories had produced 6,590 tanks and 15,735 aircraft. However, Soviet industry was concentrated in the

⬇ **Workers build tanks in a Soviet factory in the Ural Mountains.**

HOME GUARD

The Home Guard was Britain's civil defense force. It was created by Winston Churchill in May 1940, when Britain faced the prospect of a German invasion. More than a million volunteers—usually older men and those who were exempt from full military service—served in anti-aircraft units or carried out other duties. The British knew them as "Dad's Army."

KEY THEMES

west of the country, making the factories vulnerable to a German invasion from the west. As the Germans pushed east after the surprise invasion of Russia, Soviet workers dismantled 2,500 factories, moved all the equipment by road and rail, and rebuilt the factories far to the east in the Ural Mountains. Around 80 percent of Soviet war industry was saved.

As many as 25 million people may have traveled east to the Urals to work. In 1944 alone, Soviet factories produced 40,200 aircraft and 29,000 tanks. This home-grown production was helped by the Lend-Lease scheme, under which the Soviet's allies, the United States, supplied them with 22,000 aircraft and 12,500 tanks.

KEY THEMES

WOMEN IN THE SOVIET UNION

In February 1942 the Soviet government decided to allow women to be drafted into war service. By 1945, 55 percent of Soviet civilian workers were female. Women were some of the best-trained workers in the country. Some 800,000 Soviet women also had combat roles, serving as snipers and fighter pilots.

The Hardships of Daily Life

In other areas of the Soviet economy, shortages were common. Clothes were in short supply. Food production fell until the average calorie intake was around 1,000 calories per day per person, less than half the usual amount. Workers labored for up to 16 hours a day, seven days a week. With most men away at the front, and with heavy equipment such as tractors and half of all horses diverted for military use, farmers had to work for up to 20 hours a day. It was common for people rather than horses to pull plows.

← A hungry man and woman search for food near a bombed out Soviet factory.

million Soviet citizens died between 1939 and 1945, of whom more than half were civilians. This compares with 300,000 Americans and 300,000 Britons. Despite their losses, however, none of the major Allied nations considered giving up on the war because of hardships at home.

Meanwhile, Stalin did not tolerate any criticism of his policies. He sent any critics to remote prison camps called gulags, or had them executed.

Life in the Soviet Union

Conditions were at their worst in areas of the Soviet Union under German occupation. Nazi execution squads killed Communist Party officials, Jews, and any resistance fighters. Around 1,700 Soviet cities were destroyed or damaged by German bombing. In all, up to 25

→ This poster urges Russians to join the army to defeat the Germans who have invaded their homeland.

AXIS HOME FRONTS

For the citizens of Germany, Italy, and Japan, the aggression of their leaders had a devastating effect on everyday life.

At the very start of the war, the German people saw little sign of the change that would come to their standard of living. The Nazi government had increased the numbers of civil servant jobs, and salaries were high. Things seemed to be going well.

Deepening Crisis

The rapid German military victories of 1939 and 1940 hid a weak German economy, however. Hitler had prepared for a quick war (*Blitzkrieg*), and did not have the resources for a long, drawn-out war. In addition, by 1941 his armies were stretched from Scandinavia to Libya and from the English Channel to Moscow. War on such a huge scale depended on

➔ A cart in Ukraine carries vital provisions of grain destined for the people of Germany.

⬇ German civilians used these ration coupons to buy bread, butter, meat, and cereal grains.

vast reserves of manpower, raw materials, and money. Rationing, which began in 1939, started to hit home for the first time. Food, coal, soap, and gasoline were all rationed.

Women Join the War

In 1939 the German workforce included 37 percent women. However, the Nazi Party believed that women should be homemakers, and the numbers of women in work fell when the Nazis came to power. In February 1942, Albert Speer became minister for war production and switched the economy to war production.

RATIONING IN GERMANY

At the start of the war, food rations in Germany were generous. They included unlimited bread, for example. By October 1942, however, rations had been drastically cut. They were reduced more as the war turned against Germany. At the end of the war, they were less than a third of what they had been in 1939. In the face of such restrictions, the black market flourished.

KEY THEMES

→ German civilians and members of the militaristic Hitler Youth organization wait to perform compulsory labor.

Facing a severe shortage of male workers because so many men were fighting on the Eastern Front, Speer ordered women to go to work in the armaments industries. By 1944, women made up more than 50 percent of the civilian German workforce.

On February 18, 1943, following the Soviet defeat of the Germans at Stalingrad, Joseph Goebbels, the Nazi propaganda minister, announced that Germany would have to fight a "total war." Every male civilian between the ages of 16 and 65 years had to be put to work for the state. Later that same year, boys as young as 15 manned antiaircraft guns around German cities. Some 7.8 million foreign workers also worked for the Germans, often as slave laborers.

As a result of such measures, German industrial production of hardware such as tanks and military aircraft increased by about tenfold between 1939 and 1944. It was only in the last few months of the war, when the Allies invaded Germany from the west and the east, that industrial output fell.

"Having to go to work over piles of rubble and through clouds of dust; the impossibility of washing oneself properly or of cooking because there was no water, gas, or electricity; the difficulty of shopping because most of the shops had been destroyed; the delay in postal deliveries, the stopping of newspapers."

U.S. report on the difficulties of daily life in Aachen, Germany

OPPOSITION TO THE NAZIS

The Nazis suppressed all opposition, but there were still some anti-Nazi movements inside Germany. In 1942, brother and sister Sophie and Hans Scholl started the White Rose Group to oppose the Nazis. They were both executed. During the war, there were numerous plots against Hitler. In July 1944 a bomb plot by senior military officers narrowly missed killing him.

Propaganda and Morale

The Nazis used propaganda to reinforce national unity. Goebbels staged great public rallies to convince people of German military supremacy even in the face of huge defeats such as Stalingrad in the winter of 1942–1943. Propaganda could not lessen the impact of the Allied bombing campaign, however. The campaign grew more intensive after 1942, and cities such as Dresden and

← A large workforce of German women was involved in making military uniforms.

Hamburg were flattened. A total of 305,000 German civilians died in Allied bombing raids; five million were left homeless and 800,000 were injured.

Near the end of the war, when defeat became inevitable, Germans faced increasing brutality from their own government. The Nazi police and SS organizations locked up or executed anyone critical of Hitler's regime.

Life in Italy

Italians also suffered from rationing, poor wages, long working hours, and Allied bombing. Most Italians were far less committed to the war than the Germans, however. While the Nazi Party imposed unity on the German people, Benito Mussolini's fascist regime divided Italy.

Italy had two distinctive regions. The north was wealthier, with industrial cities such as Milan and Turin. The agricultural south was much poorer. The war made life worse in both north and south. Around two million Italian men were drafted into the armed forces to fight with their Axis allies. Many Italians were killed or captured in North Africa or on the Eastern Front.

At home, taxation rose and wages fell. In nonmilitary industries, unemployment rose sharply, but this was offset by war factories, which needed more workers. Working conditions were very poor and in March 1943 the country was gripped by a series of major strikes and sugar, soap, food, and clothing were severely rationed. Families relied on the illegal black market to feed themselves.

→ The Allies criticized
Pope Pius XII for not doing
enough to condemn the
Nazis and the fascists.

Italy Changes Sides

When the Allies invaded Sicily on July 10, 1943, the Italian government turned against Mussolini, who was fired by King Victor Emmanuel III. The Italians signed an armistice, or truce, with the Allies on September 3. Furious, the Germans raced to occupy Italy. By the end of July, the Germans controlled Italy north of Naples while the Allies controlled the south.

Life was hard on both sides of the line. The Germans sent Italian Jews to death camps. Other Italians were recruited for forced labor. Partisans—unofficial armed forces—attacked the occupiers, but about 40,000 partisans died fighting the Germans. In the south, the Allies seized food supplies, causing hunger and starvation. The Allied bombing of Naples had also left 200,000 citizens homeless.

Life in Japan

Japan had been at war since the early 1930s, when it began a long conflict with China. By 1940, 66 percent of Japan's total economy was used for the

POPE PIUS XII

In 1933 the Italian Cardinal Eugenio Pacelli agreed to maintain good relations with Germany. When he became Pope Pius XII in 1939, he continued to deal with the Nazi regime. His role remains controversial. He said little on the subject of the Holocaust, although he did criticize the murder of the Jews in general terms. The pope's aid organizations also saved the lives of many Jews.

JAPANESE YOUTH

As in Germany, Japan mobilized its young people for the war effort. The Greater Japan Youth Corps (GJYC) took control of all schools in 1941. Book learning became less important than military-style training. Children learned military theory and anti-Western history. Near the end of the war, large numbers of these young people volunteered to fight for their country.

ships—slowly strangled the economy by cutting off Japan's supply of imports. In 1945, the economy collapsed completely, causing social chaos. People fled from the devastating U.S. air raids on the cities, leaving industry without many of its key workers.

As shortages grew worse, the Japanese government and other bodies tried to warn the Japanese people about the sacrifices necessary to win the war. Society became more militarized.

military. Japan lacked any of its own natural resources, so when war began the government found it difficult to import essential goods, such as petrol, rice, and metals. However, it was still able to increase its military production. In 1941, 5,088 aircraft were produced; in 1944, the figure was 28,180.

Economic and Social Collapse

As the war went on, U.S. naval and air power—particularly an effective submarine campaign against merchant

→ A Tokyo businessman travels by bicycle taxi. There was not enough gasoline for all cars.

→ This Italian poster shows a U.S. "gangster" and an Italian child killed by Allied bombing.

After the Battle of Midway in 1942, Japan was on the defensive. The government widened conscription to include all males, and from September 1943 conscripted single women to work in agriculture and industry. Still the Japanese faced hunger or starvation. By the end of 1944, food rations were just a handful of

I DELITTI INUMANI DEI "GANGSTERS PILOTI" RADIANO PER SEMPRE GLI STATI UNITI DAL CONSORZIO CIVILE

vegetables and 8 oz (225 g) of rice per person. In the last months of the war, there was no rice. People ate cats and dogs. Starvation and disease were rampant. Allied bombings also destroyed morale. In one raid on Tokyo on March 9, 1945, more than 100,000 people died.

At the start of the war, the Axis powers were not prepared for a long conflict against the industrial might of the United States. Their civilians paid dearly for their leaders' ambitions.

OCCUPATION AND RESISTANCE

Enemy occupation brought hardship and deprivation to countries in Europe and Asia. Many people lived in fear, though others welcomed their new rulers.

By the end of 1942, rapid German and Japanese conquests had created huge empires across Europe and Southeast Asia. For millions of people on both continents, this meant living at home under the control of a foreign military government that was often highly repressive.

Nazi Control in Europe

The German government controlled vast swathes of Europe. The citizens of France, Belgium, the Netherlands, Luxembourg, Poland, Denmark, Norway, Finland, Estonia, Latvia, Lithuania, Yugoslavia, Greece, northern Italy, Ukraine, parts of Russia, and parts of North Africa found themselves living under Axis occupation.

Life under Axis rule varied widely from country to country. The Nazis ruled some countries directly from Berlin; other

← Czechs study a poster calling for volunteers for the SS, the elite Nazi security service.

MARSHAL PETAIN

Philippe Pétain was the head of state of the French Vichy government. A popular hero from World War I, he argued against resisting the German take-over. Pétain set up a collaborationist government at Vichy in central France. After the war, the French tried him as a war criminal. He was found guilty and sentenced to death. In the end, he was reprieved, but he spent the rest of his life as a prisoner.

KEY PEOPLE

← A resistance fighter from the French Maquis shows his compatriots how to strip and clean a Sten gun.

countries were placed under the control of a Reich governor, who was a senior Nazi answering directly to Hitler. Some other countries were placed under a civil administration that would enforce Nazi laws, or they might be under direct military rule by the German Army.

The most repressive forms of occupation came in Eastern Europe, where countries were under military rule (as were northern and western France). The Netherlands was governed by the Netherlands Reich

← Danes wear Jewish skull caps in the colors of the British RAF as a protest against German occupation.

The Germans taxed occupied countries heavily, making them pay for the price of occupation. The Germans also took food and other resources. In France, shortages were normal because the best food was kept for the occupiers. The French made coffee from acorns because the Germans took all the real coffee. In Denmark, the Germans took so much of the harvest that the Danish people starved.

Any attack on a German soldier or official was met with severe reprisals. In a few cases, that involved the killing of a whole village in revenge for the death of one German. When Czech partisans killed Reinhard Heydrich, the Nazi governor of Bohemia and Moravia, the village of Lidice was destroyed and its population killed or sent to death camps.

Commission, while Denmark kept its elected government and monarchy but both institutions were entirely controlled by the Germans.

Occupied Life

The Germans issued their subjects in occupied countries with official identity papers they had to carry at all times. Nightly curfews were usual. Anyone who was found outside during the hours of the curfew, or who broke other rules, could be imprisoned or even executed.

Collaborating with the Enemy

In countries such as Belgium, people and authorities collaborated with their Nazi rulers on a daily basis. They hoped this would spare the country from the worst excesses of Nazi rule. Some collaborators were more enthusiastic, however. They supported Nazi principles and actively helped the Germans. Some French women had children with German soldiers. In Vichy France, politicians helped deport French Jews to Nazi concentration camps. In Norway, the government followed fascist policies.

Resistance

Many people living in occupied countries deeply resented their Axis rulers and did everything they could to resist them.

⬇ A member of the Milice, the pro-Nazi military police in France, helps round up suspected Resistance fighters.

❝Nothing could make me accept that this new order of things will be just, moral, and human. One sees injustice, immorality, and inhumanity, thieving, the plundering of every living thing by the invaders in order to make the population die of hunger, terror, and police brutality.❞

Mario Rigouzzo
French consul in occupied Greece, February 1943

EYEWITNESS ACCOUNT

➔ Members of the Indian National Army celebrate their declaration of war on the Allies in October 1943.

The most famous resistance movement was the Maquis, or French Resistance. It played a key role in the preparations for D-Day in June 1944, blowing up miles of railroad lines and supplying the Allies with information about German defenses. In Norway, the armed resistance movement had 40,000 members. Trained by the British, their most important action was to blow up a factory that was part of Germany's atomic bomb plans in 1943.

KEY EVENTS

THE INDIAN NATIONAL ARMY

Before the war, the Indian nationalist Subhas Chandra Bose had tried to make an alliance with Adolf Hitler to overthrow British rule in India. During the war, it was Japan that offered Bose the support he needed to recruit 40,000 men for the Indian National Army (INA), mainly from among prisoners of war and Indian expatriates. The INA fought the Allies in Burma.

In Eastern Europe, there were large resistance movements in Poland, Russia, and Yugoslavia. In Warsaw, the Polish capital, there were two huge risings against the German occupiers in 1943 and 1944. The German troops put the risings down with great brutality. In Russia and Yugoslavia, former soldiers formed partisan groups. These were unofficial groups who wore a kind of uniform and adopted a form of military organization. The Allied governments supplied the partisans in Yugoslavia with arms and money. A similar movement emerged in Italy after the Germans took control in Italy in September 1943.

Japanese Occupation

For the Japanese, meanwhile, occupying their neighbors was a means of getting the raw materials they needed that could not be produced at home, such as food and oil. Japanese military governments took over in Hong Kong, Singapore, Borneo, New Guinea, and present-day Indonesia. Some countries— Burma and French Indochina—were allowed to keep their own governments. The Japanese rewarded Thailand for its support by giving it territory taken from Burma and Malaya. Some Asian politicians, particularly in Burma and India, welcomed the Japanese as liberators from British colonial rule.

Life under Japanese occupation was hardest in China, much of which had been occupied since 1937. A number of Japanese atrocities against Chinese citizens included the so-called Rape of Nanking in 1937, when the Japanese murdered half of the 600,000 inhabitants of Nanking, the former Chinese capital. The Chinese had to wear identity badges and bow to passing Japanese soldiers. Failure to do so was punishable by death. The Japanese took so much of China's rice harvest that starvation became common among the Chinese.

The British and Americans trained guerrilla groups across Southeast Asia to resist Japanese occupation. The most successful group was the Malayan People's Anti-Japanese Army, which had 7,000 members. They attacked Japanese soldiers and officials. The treatment of anyone who questioned Japanese authority was cruel, however. As a result, resistance by individuals was usually limited and mostly ineffective.

← European women do chores in a Japanese internment camp in Singapore.

THE HOLOCAUST

Away from the public gaze, a hidden tragedy was taking place. Millions of innocent people were being murdered by the Nazis in the name of racial purity.

The Holocaust is the name given to the Nazi attempt to exterminate the Jewish people. The Nazis murdered an estimated six million Jews, as well as hundreds of thousands of non-Jewish victims, mainly in Poland and Russia. The non-Jewish victims included gypsies (Roma), homosexuals, communists, and the mentally ill.

Hitler's Beliefs

When Adolf Hitler and the Nazis first came to power in Germany in 1933, it seemed likely he would make life difficult for Germany's large Jewish community. Hitler had made his hatred of the Jews clear in *Mein Kampf* (My Struggle), his 1924 book that outlined his political beliefs. Hitler blamed Germany's defeat in World War I on an international Jewish conspiracy.

➡ A young Nazi puts up a notice telling people to boycott Jewish stores.

↑ The windows of this Jewish store in Berlin were smashed on *Kristallnacht* in November 1938.

Hitler's belief struck a chord with many Germans. Anti-Semitism, or a hatred of Jews, had a long history in parts of central and Eastern Europe. The Nazis wanted to create an Aryan (Germanic) super race, which meant eliminating all "inferior" races.

The First Steps

Soon after coming to power in 1933, the Nazi Party set about this eradication. The first "inferior" people to be affected were not Jews but people suffering from hereditary illnesses. They were sterilized to stop them having children.

Then the Nazis turned to the Jews. More than half a million Jews lived in Germany. Nazi activists attacked Jews and damaged their shops. Jewish lawyers and doctors were not allowed to practice. In September 1935, harsher laws were introduced to discriminate

REINHARD HEYDRICH

Senior Nazi general Reinhard Heydrich was a key architect of the Holocaust. In 1939 he took control of the Reich Security Main Office. The office provided central control for SS and police terror activities in Germany and occupied territories. Heydrich organized the special mobile killing units (*Einsatzgruppen*). He also oversaw the building of extermination camps. At the Wannsee Conference in January 1942, Heydrich took charge of plans for the "Final Solution." He was murdered by Czech partisans four months later.

KEY PEOPLE

against Jews. These included banning marriage between Jews and non-Jews and stripping Jews of German citizenship. The laws aimed to separate Jews from the rest of society. Many Jews fled from Germany to other countries.

Kristallnacht

On the night of November 9/10, 1938, Nazi propaganda minister Joseph Goebbels unleashed mobs of party activists against German Jews. They attacked Jewish businesses and burned synagogues. Some 20,000 Jews were detained in what were known as concentration camps. The attacks became known as *Kristallnacht* (Crystal Night or Night of the Broken Glass) because of the smashed windows of Jewish stores. The Nazis thought the attacks would be popular among the Germans, but many people were shocked and appalled by the violence. The Nazi leadership decided that in future they would have to deal with the Jews away from public gaze.

⬇ `People trade their used clothes in the snow in a Jewish ghetto in Poland.`

← A mother in Ukraine shields her child as a member of an *Einsatzgruppe* prepares to fire.

Nazi ideology were virtually subhuman and more hated than the German Jews. Hitler wanted to remove them to give the German people *Lebensraum* or "living room." Many Polish Jews were killed by mobile killing units called *Einsatzgruppen* who followed the main troops. Others were forced into ghettos, where they died from overwork, starvation, and disease. With the German conquests in Scandinavia, Western Europe, and the Balkans in 1940 and 1941, still more Jews came under Nazi control.

The First Concentration Camps

Since coming to power in 1933, the Nazis had used concentration camps to detain their political opponents, such as communists. But from 1938, more people were sent to the camps, including many Jews, and the conditions in the camps worsened. The SS—the *Schutzstaffel*, the Nazi Party's racial elite—used the inmates to provide labor for its own industrial enterprises. The SS built new camps near factories where inmates were forced to work as slaves. In the harsh conditions, many were worked to death.

The Nazis in Europe

With the defeat of Poland in September 1939, some 2.5 million Jews came under Nazi rule. Polish Jews were Slavs, which in

EINSATZGRUPPEN

The *Einsatzgruppen* (special task forces) were mobile military police units who carried out the mass murder of the Nazis' racial and political enemies. They were first used in Poland in 1939. By the time Hitler invaded the Soviet Union in June 1941, they numbered about 3,000 men. They used army units and local people to round up their victims, who were shot. In the Soviet Union, they killed at least 700,000 people.

KEY THEMES

ADOLF EICHMANN

Adolf Eichmann worked for Reinhard Heydrich and later for the Gestapo. In 1939 he organized the deportation of Jews to Poland. He later implemented the "Final Solution." In August 1944 he reported to Heinrich Himmler, head of the SS, that four million Jews had died in the death camps and another two million had been killed by mobile extermination units.

Operation Barbarossa

In June 1941, the Germans invaded the Soviet Union. Hitler saw the invasion, code-named Operation Barbarossa, as a "war of annihilation." He believed that the Jews were behind communism and that by defeating the Soviets he could destroy both communism and the Jews.

Within a few months of Operation Barbarossa, the Germans reorganized their entire campaign against the Jews. Heinrich Himmler, head of the SS, had set up the first concentration camp at Dachau, Germany, in 1933. Hitler appointed him Reich commissar for the strengthening of German Racial Identity.

↑ Adolf Eichmann fled to Latin America after the war, but was captured by Israeli agents, tried, and hanged in 1962.

Now Himmler was in charge of Poland and his deputy, Reinhard Heydrich, was made head of the Gestapo, the criminal police and the Security Service. Between them, two men now had the power to implement the extermination of the Jews.

In October 1941, four months after the invasion of the Soviet Union, Heydrich organized the mass deportation of Jews from Germany, Austria, and Poland to the "General Government." The General

Government was part of Poland that the Germans ran as an independent colony. The arrival of the newcomers created huge Jewish ghettos in Polish cities such as Lödz and Warsaw.

Nazis in Germany demanded to have all Jews removed from the Reich. With the ghettos in Poland full, however, the killing squads of the *Einsatzgruppen* could not kill all the Jews arriving in the General Government. The senior Nazi leaders decided that they needed a new way to kill Jewish prisoners more quickly.

On July 31, 1941, Himmler authorized Reinhard Heydrich to find a "final solution to the Jewish question." The order authorized Heydrich to take any steps necessary to organize the mass extermination of the Jews. By December 1941, mobile "gas vans" were being used to kill Jews with poisonous gas.

The Wannsee Conference

On January 20, 1942, Heydrich organized a conference in the Berlin suburb of Wannsee where senior Nazis discussed the practicalities of the "Final Solution" and finalized their plans. By the end of March 1942, the mass extermination of Poland's Jewish population was underway in specially constructed death camps such as Belzec, Sobibor, and Treblinka. The most notorious extermination camp of all, Auschwitz-Birkenau, began its mass gassings of Jews and others in June 1942.

← Railroad tracks run up to the entrance to the death camp at Auschwitz-Birkenau.

→ This crematorium was used to burn bodies at the concentration camp at Dachau.

Role of Local People

In some occupied countries, local people helped the Germans, either by killing Jews or by deporting them to the death camps. Lithuanians, Romanians, and Ukrainians all took part in the destruction of their large Jewish populations. However, while the Vichy government in France cooperated in rounding up Jews, many French people hid Jews to protect them. The Dutch protested deportations of Jews, while the Danes helped get most

MEDICAL EXPERIMENTS

Nazi doctors used camp inmates for horrifying experiments. Among other tests, they exposed victims to extreme cold. They wanted to find out how long it took to freeze to death. They wanted to help prevent the deaths of German airmen and sailors by freezing. Jewish victims were put in ice water or left naked in subzero temperatures.

Danish Jews to safety in neutral Sweden. Finland, Italy, and Hungary also refused to hand over any Jews, although up to 15 percent of Italian Jews were deported after the Germans occupied the northern part of Italy in 1943 and Hungary also cooperated later in the war.

Inside the Death Camps

The death camps were small and simple. For example, Treblinka covered 315,000 square yards (270 sqm). It was run by just 50 Germans and 150 Ukrainians, with 1,000 Jews to help sort the bodies. But more than 800,000 Jews died in the camp. The victims were transported to the camps by rail. They were crammed into cattle trucks in which many

The death camps were grossly effective. The vast majority of Jews in eastern Europe were killed in 1942 and 1943. Later, Jews from Western Europe and Hungary were also killed. By the end of the war in 1945, the Nazis had killed an estimated six million Jews, 500,000 homosexuals, and 250,000 Roma. This genocide is now known as the Holocaust, from a Greek phrase for an animal burned as a sacrifice to the gods. Jews often refer to it as *Shoah*, a Hebrew word that means "calamity."

suffocated. When they arrived at the camp, men and women were separated. Those who could not work—the young, the old, and the weak—were told to undress. Their clothes and valuables were taken away. The naked prisoners were ordered into what appeared to be a shower block but which was actually a gas chamber. The doors were bolted, the room sealed, and the gas turned on. After the victims were dead, Jewish guards buried or burned their bodies.

→ Half-starved prisoners are taken to the hospital after liberation in May 1945.

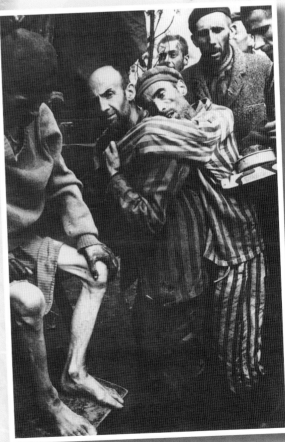

TIMELINE OF WORLD WAR II

1939 | **September:** German troops invade and overrun Poland; Britain and France declare war on Germany; the Soviet Union invades eastern Poland. The Battle of the Atlantic begins.

April: Germany invades Denmark and Norway; Allied troops land in Norway.

May: Germany invades Luxembourg, the Netherlands, Belgium, and France; Allied troops are evacuated at Dunkirk.

June: Allied troops leave Norway; Italy enters the war; France signs an armistice with Germany; Italy bombs Malta in the Mediterranean.

July: German submarines (U-boats) inflict heavy losses on Allied convoys in the Atlantic; The Battle of Britain begins.

September: Luftwaffe air raids begin the Blitz—the bombing of British cities; Italian troops advance from Libya into Egypt.

October: Italy invades Greece.

December: British troops defeat the Italians at Sidi Barrani, Egypt.

1941 | **January:** Allied units capture Tobruk in Libya.

February: Rommel's Afrika Korps arrive in Tripoli.

March: The Afrika Korps drive British troops back from El Agheila.

April: Axis units invade Yugoslavia; German forces invade Greece; the Afrika Korps besiege Tobruk.

June: German troops invade the Soviet Union.

September: Germans besiege Leningrad and attack Moscow.

December: Japanese aircraft attack the U.S. Pacific Fleet at Pearl Harbor; Japanese forces invade the Philippines, Malaya, and Thailand, and defeat the British garrison in Hong Kong.

1942 | **January:** Japan invades Burma; Rommel launches a new offensive in Libya; Allied troops leave Malaya.

February: Singapore surrenders to the Japanese.

April: The Bataan Peninsula in the Philippines falls to the Japanese.

May: U.S. and Japanese fleets clash at the Battle of the Coral Sea.

June: The U.S. Navy defeats the Japanese at the Battle of Midway; Rommel recaptures Tobruk.

September–October: Allied forces defeat Axis troops at El Alamein, Egypt, the first major Allied victory of the war.

November: U.S. and British troops land in Morocco and Algeria.

1943

February: The German Sixth Army surrenders at Stalingrad; the Japanese leave Guadalcanal in the Solomon Islands.

May: Axis forces in Tunisia surrender.

July: The Red Army wins the Battle of Kursk; Allied troops land on the Italian island of Sicily.

August: German forces occupy Italy; the Soviets retake Kharkov.

September: Allied units begin landings on mainland Italy; Italy surrenders, prompting a German invasion of northern Italy.

November: U.S. carrier aircraft attack Rabaul in the Solomon Islands.

1944

January: The German siege of Leningrad ends.

February: U.S. forces conquer the Marshall Islands.

March: The Soviet offensive reaches the Dniester River; Allied aircraft bomb the monastery at Monte Cassino in Italy.

June: U.S. troops enter the city of Rome; D-Day–the Allied invasion of northern Europe; U.S. aircraft defeat the Japanese fleet at the Battle of the Philippine Sea.

July: Soviet tanks enter Poland.

August: Japanese troops retreat in Burma; Allied units liberate towns in France, Belgium, and the Netherlands.

October: The Japanese suffer defeat at the Battle of Leyte Gulf.

December: German troops counterattack in the Ardennes.

1945

January: The U.S. Army lands on Luzon in the Philippines; most of Poland and Czechoslovakia are liberated by the Allies.

February: U.S. troops land on Iwo Jima; Soviet troops strike west across Germany; the U.S. Army heads toward the Rhine River.

April: U.S. troops land on the island of Okinawa; Mussolini is shot by partisans; Soviet troops assault Berlin; Hitler commits suicide.

May: All active German forces surrender.

June: Japanese resistance ends in Burma and on Okinawa.

August: Atomic bombs are dropped on Hiroshima and Nagasaki; Japan surrenders.

GLOSSARY

Allies One of the two groups of combatants in the war. The main Allies were Britain, the Soviet Union, the United States, British Empire troops, and free forces from occupied nations.

air-raid shelter A reinforced place for people to shelter from a bomb attack.

armistice An agreement made by both sides in a war to stop fighting for a time.

atrocities Extremely wicked or inhuman acts.

Axis One of the two groups of combatants in the war. The leading Axis powers were Germany, Italy, and Japan.

blackout A period when all lights must be turned off or covered up.

boycott To avoid buying goods from a particular source as a form of protest.

civil defense Measures by civilians to avoid or counter attacks during wartime.

collaborating Working together with an occupying government.

conscription The compulsory enlistment of people into the armed services.

conspiracy A secret plan for a group of people to do something illegal or harmful.

curfew A law requiring people to stay indoors, usually at night.

deported Forcibly expelled from a country.

drafted Forced to join the military or another organization.

Einstazgruppen Mobile killing units of the Security Police and SS Security Service.

evacuated Sent to a different place for reasons of safety.

fascist Someone who believes in a dictatorial, militaristic political system.

final solution A term for the Nazi attempt to exterminate Europe's Jews.

Holocaust A term for the Nazi attempt to exterminate Europe's Jews.

intern To confine or imprison a civilian during wartime.

Kistallnacht The "Night of Broken Glass," when Nazis attacked Jewish property in Germany in November 1938.

Lebensraum German for "living space," Hitler's policy of grabbing land in eastern Europe.

militarism A political belief that military concerns should shape society, which should be organized with strict rules and discipline.

occupation The seizure and control of an area by military force.

partisans Members of armed groups that secretly fight an occupying enemy force.

propaganda Material and information presented in a way intended to improve morale or damage enemy morale.

SS An abbreviation for Schutzstaffel, the elite military security force of the Nazi Party.

FURTHER RESOURCES

Books

Adams, Simon. *Occupation and Resistance* (Documenting World War II). Rosen Central, 2008.

Adams, Simon. *Holocaust* (World War Two). Sea to Sea Publications, 2009.

Colman, Penny. *Rosie the Riveter: Women Working on the Home Front in World War II*. Random House Children's Books, 2009.

Gitlin, Martin. *World War II on the Home Front: An Interactive History Adventure* (You Choose). Capstone Press, 2012.

Samuels, Charlie. *Home Front* (World War II Sourcebooks). Brown Bear Books, 2012.

Samuels, Charlie. *Life Under Occupation* (World War II Sourcebooks). Brown Bear Books, 2012.

Wiener, Tom. *Voices of War: Stories of Service from the Home Front and the Front Lines*. San Val, 2005.

Websites

http://www.history.com/topics/ world-war-ii/us-home-front-during- world-war-ii
Links to pages about the U.S. home front from the History Channel.

www.historyonthenet.com/ww2/ home_front.htm
Historyonthenet.com page of links about the British home front in World War II.

http://www.ushmm.org/wlc/en/ article.php?ModuleId=10007653
Timeline of the Holocaust from the United States Holocaust Memorial Museum.

http://www.pbs.org/thewar/
PBS pages on the war to support the Ken Burns' film, *The War*.

http://www.ameshistory.org/ exhibits/events/rationing.htm
Online exhibition about rationing in the United States during the war.

INDEX